The
Hungry
Fox
Tasty treats
By Cole Adams

"It is spring again. The earth is like a child that knows poems by heart."

— Rainer Maria Rilke

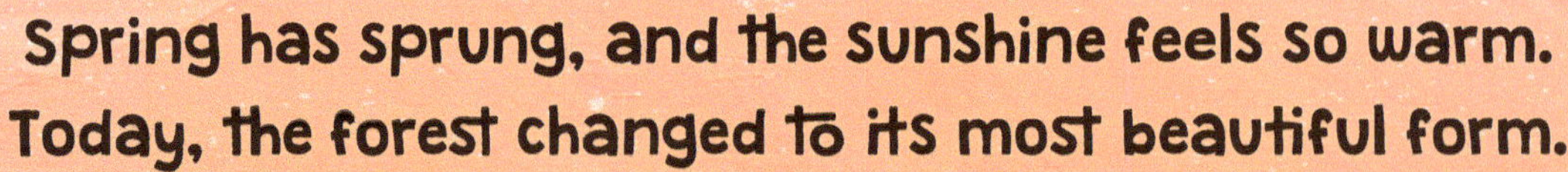

Spring has sprung, and the sunshine feels so warm.
Today, the forest changed to its most beautiful form.

Greeneries, flowers, and roses are everywhere you see,
and colorful birds chirp with joy and glee.

They chant to anyone near to hear,
that no one goes hungry this time of year.

Because unlike winter season when food is rare,
spring is a completely different affair.

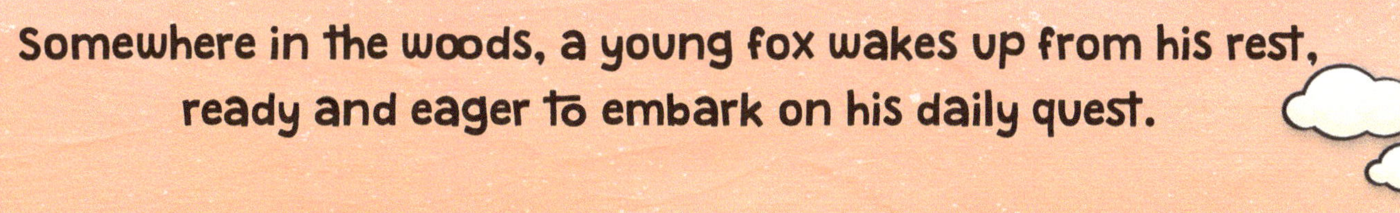

Somewhere in the woods, a young fox wakes up from his rest,
ready and eager to embark on his daily quest.

Which is to fill his belly with delicious food before bedtime,
while paying a visit to his neighbors that talk in rhyme.

Last winter season, they all did him one big favor,
by helping him change his bad behavior.

And so today, the much more behaved fox starts his day,
by wondering what new adventure awaits him along the way.

The Fox and the Snake

Not long after sunrise, the fox ventured into the beautiful forest with an empty stomach and a heart full of hope. He strolled cheerfully for a while, stopping only to admire the flowers that always lit his face with a big, goofy smile. After sniffing more flowers than he could count, he came across something that was kind of a surprise—he had found a pile of watermelons of an astonishing size!

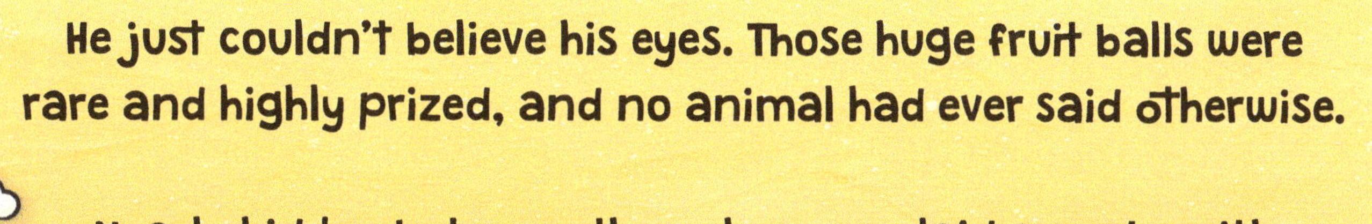

He just couldn't believe his eyes. Those huge fruit balls were rare and highly prized, and no animal had ever said otherwise.

Nearly hidden between them, however, laid a snake with glistening, green skin. He was all curled up and he could have been mistaken for one of the melons—like he was in disguise. He laid still until he felt the fox approach, then lifted his head and slowly started to rise.

"Hello there, my furry friend," said the snake with a grin on his face. "I see you're salivating over my famous bounty."

"I can't say that I'm not," admitted the fox in all honesty.

"I'm giving them away, in a way..." added the snake strangely while starting to sway.

"Whoa!" exclaimed the fox. "It seems like today will be my lucky day."

"Almost..." added the snake mysteriously. "Only if we can come to an agreement that would benefit you and me."

The fox felt very suspicious of the snake but thought it wouldn't hurt to hear his proposal. So, he accepted to hear him out eventually.

"Here's my condition," said the snake. "For you to take a melon, bring me something rare that neither grows on trees, nor on the ground."

"Consider it done," replied the fox hastily, not sure if such a thing could be found.

"I'll be waiting right here," stated the snake before curling back on the floor and disappearing between the watermelons like before.

The fox, on the other hand, stepped away and continued on his way–puzzled by the snake's request. This was surely one of the oddest encounters he had on all his quests.

The Fox and the Badger

From far away, the fox noticed a little cornfield with beautiful green stalks of amazing height. The corn ears were so big and bright that they seemed to shine under the sunlight. Just in front of them stood a badger whose fur coat was all black and white. Right when she noticed the fox, the badger waved at him to approach the site, and he gratefully accepted her invite.

"Wow, congratulations on your lovely corn farm," said
the fox while greeting the badger with a paw sign.

"Thank you, thank you..." the badger gloomily replied.
"Yeah, corn is fine..."

"Someone is overjoyed," joked the fox. "Come on, I'd be
jumping for joy if this was all mine."

"Well, I'm bored of eating just corn," replied the badger.
"I crave something sweet and divine."

The fox noticed that the badger was truly feeling blue
which made him feel a little sad, too. He wanted to help,
but he had no clue what to do. So, he simply asked:
"Tell me at least how I can help you?"

"Ooh, can you?" asked the badger curiously.

"Sure, if there's anything I can do..." he replied.

"Ooh! Ooh!" shouted the badger who was now literally
jumping up and down. "Thank you!"

Immediately, the badger ran to her beautiful field and disappeared for a while. Moments later, she reappeared with an armful of corn that she placed in front of the fox in one plentiful pile.

The fox, although very tempted, gently pushed the corn and smiled.

"I can't accept this until I help you first," he said. "So? This sweet thing? What would it be?"

"Ooh, right! Silly me. I forgot to tell you; I'm craving honey! Sweet, sweet honey from a bee."

"Whoa! That's a tough request!" exclaimed the fox. "Where would I find bees?"

"Just march east and follow the big trees," answered the badger, pointing to a path behind her. "There's a hive that you can find with ease."

And straightaway—right after saying their goodbyes—that's exactly what the fox did. He headed east and followed the big trees, making sure he picked up his speed. Perhaps he would find something rare for the snake whilst doing this good deed for the badger in need. Now that he was thinking about it again, what did the snake need? No fruits... no vegetables... maybe some kind of seed?

The Fox and the mole

Carefully following the trees and paying attention not to get lost, the fox stumbled suddenly on a particularly strange scene. In between some large trees was a little piece of land that was completely covered with holes and piles upon piles of dirt. And this time there was no greenery to be seen—only muddy earth.

"Whoa?! Who's there?" shouted a squeaky voice coming from somewhere below the ground.

The startled fox looked inside every hole but saw nothing but the freshly turned ground.

"I hear footsteps. You'd better not touch my truffles,"
said the voice again in a muffled shout.

"I do not understand what you're talking about!"
exclaimed the fox sincerely.

At that moment, a mole appeared in front of him from the
closest hole. He squinted at him with his tiny eyes for a long
time, then jumped out to sit on a stack of some roundish,
brownish, weird-looking potatoes that the fox had mistaken
for a pile of dirty rocks at first glance.

"Hey there, fox. You're telling me you know nothing about
the rarest food of the ground?" asked the mole
in a high, squeaky sound.

"No," answered the fox whose curiosity was piqued.
"I have never seen these vegetables around."

"They are more mushrooms than vegetables," corrected the
mole who had jumped back on the ground.

"Do they taste good?" asked the fox who was staring
at the strange food.

"Some animals go nuts for them,"
replied the mole."But to me,
they taste like wood."

16

Once he heard those answers, all the fox could think about was the snake's riddle. Rare mushrooms that come from below the ground sounded like the perfect food for the snake. But what would the mole want in exchange for them, wondered the fox? It was clear that he wasn't too fond of them.

"Since you don't like them, why do you collect them?" asked the fox eventually.

"Well, I always trade them for some type of grain," confessed the mole.

"Grain... grain..." repeated the fox while thinking. "Would you be interested in corn?!"

"Sweet, sun-drenched corn!. Yes, I would love to have some to nibble on."

The fox suddenly had a brilliant idea. When he finds the honey for the badger, he can trade it for corn, and trade the corn for some truffles, which—hopefully—will get him those melons he had been craving all day. This was as easy as child's play!

And so, without further delay, the fox asked the mole to save him some truffles, in exchange for corn, before continuing on his way.

The Fox and the Tortoise

Although he was starting to feel a bit tired and starved, the determined fox kept walking east. He'd just have to be patient and make some trades if he wanted to enjoy a watermelon feast.

And so, he was walking absentmindedly when his muzzle picked up on the loveliest smell. He followed the sweet odor with his eyes shut, and a smile on his face—like he was under a spell—until he bumped into something hard and fell. Then the fox opened his eyes and realized that he had slammed into a huge tortoise's shell.

"I'm so sorry," muttered the fox. "It wasn't my intention. I wasn't paying attention..."

The tortoise, who had now woken up from her nap, shrugged it off with a genuine smile.

"No worries, little fox," she said. "You were clearly distracted by the delightful fig smell."

Then, she raised her head and pointed to the fig tree that they were standing beneath. And indeed, the fox just then noticed the most beautiful and fragrant figs hanging from the tree's huge branches.

"Wow, those figs look great!" said the fox.

"The best I ever ate," added the tortoise. "But if you want to have some, you must wait."

"Why?" asked the fox while looking perplexedly at the tree.

"I can't reach those beautiful figs," answered the tortoise. "So, I wait for them to ripen and come to me."

"That sounds so boring..." said the fox with a sigh, suddenly feeling disappointed.

"It is," laughed the tortoise. "But I don't mind. I spend my time mostly sleeping and snoring."

"Maybe we could give the tree a little nudge?" proposed the fox.

"The tree trunk is too robust," said the tortoise. "Unless you shake the branches directly, those figs won't budge."

The fox looked at the enormous tree and couldn't help but frown; he couldn't think of anything to get those plump figs down.

"Don't worry about it, sweet fox," whispered the tortoise in a comforting voice. "They'll drop when they're ready."

"I'm sorry I couldn't help. I'll be back with a plan," promised the fox who thought that if he can't help, he'll look for someone who can.

And just like that, the fox left while imagining that those figs could have been a delicious snack. But he promised he'd be back. After all, they were on his track.

The Fox, The Bees & the Woodpecker

Deep into the woods and right at the end of the track lined with the big trees, the fox finally came across a hive of loud, buzzing bees. Though some were hard at work gathering pollen from every flower and rose they could see, the others were gathered in a protest around a cherry tree.

"What is wrong?" asked the fox while approaching the scene.

"That woodpecker won't stop pecking on our tree," answered one angry bee. "He disturbs our queen."

"He is very mean," added another one next to it. "Because of him, our queen is the saddest she's ever been."

The fox hadn't noticed that there was a hectic woodpecker on top of the tree, indeed. He was vigorously pecking on the trunk with incredible speed, causing the cherries to fall from their branches like tumbling beads.

"We don't know what to do," said a bee from the bee swarm. "We offered him honey but he still won't leave."

"Yes, that's true," shouted another one. "He's such a selfish peeve."

"Honey would be your reward," whispered another. "All the honey we can afford."

"Help us, please!" repeated in a choir a bunch of bees.

The fox weighed the problem, and after a moment, he had a breakthrough. Now, he knew exactly what to do. And so, he told the bees to recede from the tree while he did the opposite and got closer to it. He knocked on its trunk with his paw several times.

The woodpecker quickly ceased his pecking and looked down. "I know what you want! The bees asked you to convince me to move out," said the woodpecker. "You're wasting your time, my friend."

"Quite the contrary," lied the fox. "They just wanted me to let you know that *they're* moving out."

"Oh, where are they going to go?"

"My friend has this huge fig tree; they will settle on it and leave you be."

The bird suddenly became very interested. He started to make his way down little by little and he said: "A huge fig tree you said. Can I go instead?"

The fox couldn't believe his plan had worked. He knew the
selfish woodpecker would want the bigger fruits. He made
things easy for him. Meanwhile, the bees were jubilating
with joy. But the fox winked at them to let him
finish his ploy.

"Yes, you can," answered nonchalantly the fox.
"At the condition that the one who leaves promises not
to return here anymore."

"I promise, I promise," exclaimed the woodpecker.
"Now let's go! What are we waiting for?"

And just like that, the woodpecker flew into the sky
and waited for the fox to show him his new
home. While the bees, filled with gratitude,
thanked the fox by giving him a big chunk of
their honeycomb.

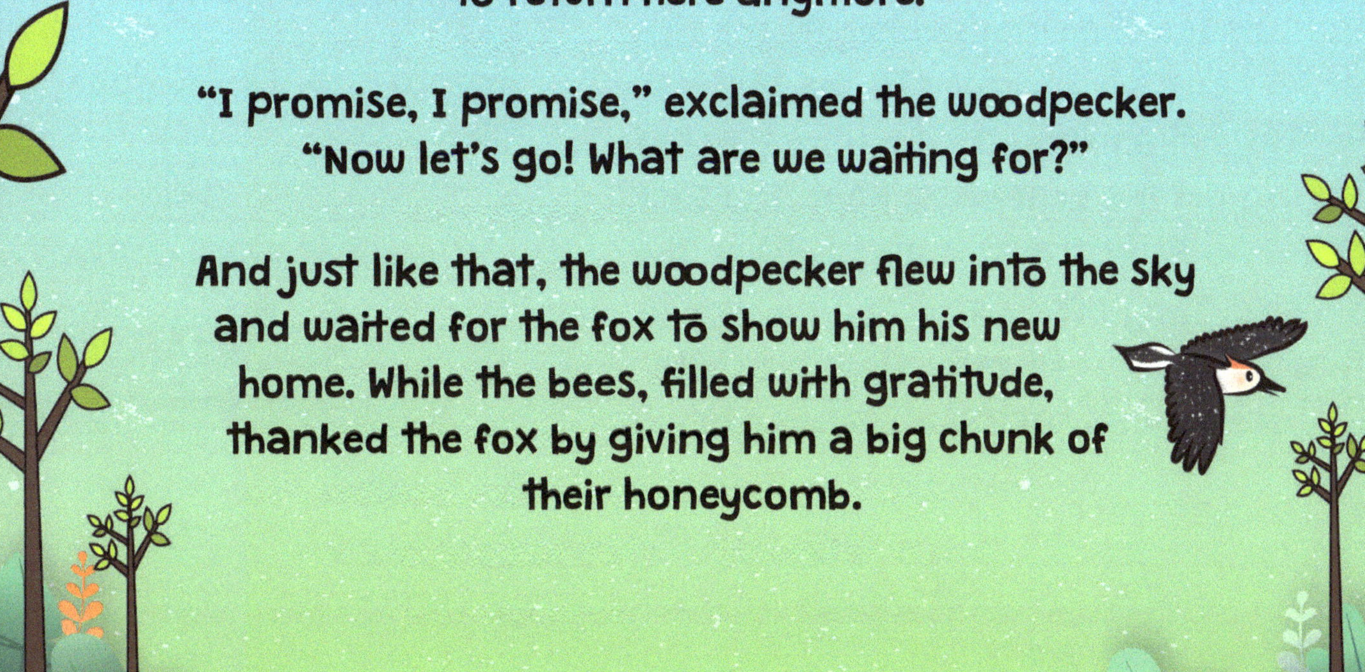

Now that the bees had returned to their honey making in peace, the fox went back on his tracks to start his trading plan and claim his prize.

First, he led the woodpecker to the fig tree to keep his promise to the tortoise. The figs fell as soon as the bird started pecking on the branches. He made such a loud noise but that didn't bother the tortoise. They offered him some figs to thank him, but he only took one bite since he was saving his appetite.

Then the fox went all the way back to the cornfield where the badger started jumping up and down like a bunny as soon as she tasted the honey.

The fox brought the corn to
the mole who took it, gave him
truffles, then vanished in a hole.

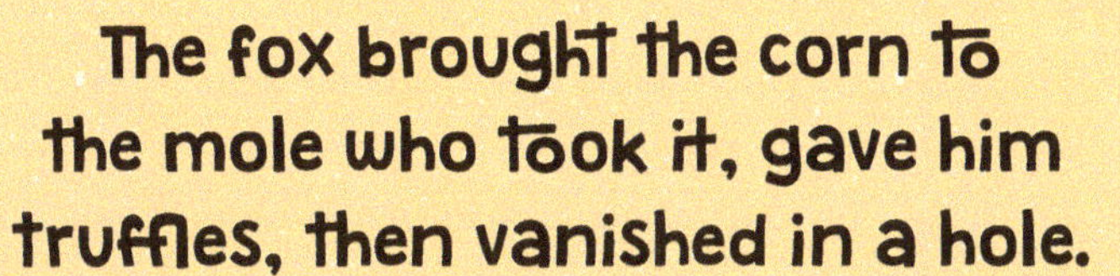

The snake ate the truffles and
thanked the fox in his hissy voice.
He was so pleased with him that
he let him pick the watermelon
of his choice.

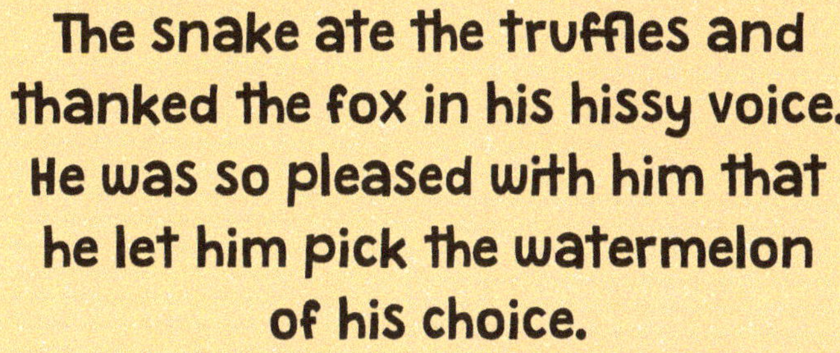

That was fun,
thought the fox after
he was done.

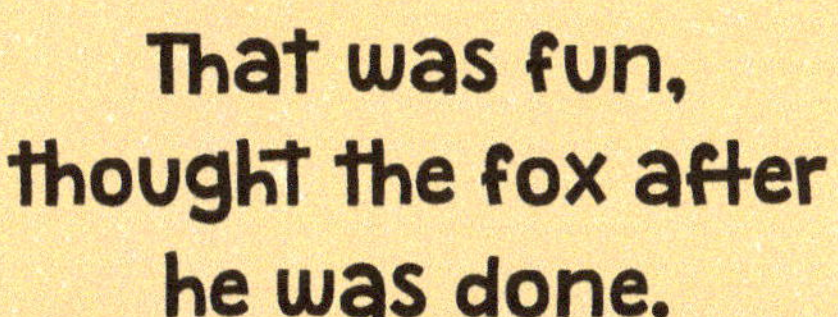

The Fox meets Felina

Although his stomach was growling for the watermelon he was carefully rolling, the fox was heading back to his den happier than he'd ever been. A few moments from now, he'd be enjoying the fruit of his dreams—or that was what he thought until he heard a scream coming from a nearby stream.

Immediately, the fox rushed towards the stream, and once
there, he found another fox standing in the running water,
with her fur completely wet. And from the look on her face,
it was clear that she was very upset.

"What happened to you?" asked the fox, jumping into
the fresh stream to help.

"I was trying to cross the stream when my watermelon
slipped from my paws and got carried away by the water,"
answered the sad vixen. "I'll never find another one.
Those things are so rare!"

"Look over there," said the fox with an amused tone.
"It just happens that I have a watermelon of my own.
I'll be happy if we can share."

"Oh, what a sweet coincidence!" she exclaimed
cheerfully. "But it wouldn't be fair for you."

"Have you seen the size of that fruit?" said jokingly the fox.
"I'm sure we can both eat from it and still have some
left to spare."

The vixen nodded her head timidly and said: "All right,
but we can share the watermelon under one condition..."

"Which is?" asked the fox swiftly.

"I need to hear the story of how you got it first," she joked. "It took me all day to find mine. I'm sure It wasn't easy for you either."

The fox laughed and said: "Funny, I was just going to ask you how you got *your* watermelon too."

"My name is Felina, by the way," said the vixen with a genuine smile.

"Nice to meet you Felina," replied the fox. "I'm Finn."

And right beside the babbling stream, under the golden setting sun, Finn and Felina sat down to tell their day-long adventures before finally sharing the watermelon—which, even for the two of them, was so much more than what they could eat. But most importantly, the great fruit was incredibly juicy and sweet—or what they loved to call: a **tasty treat!**